Forest Full
of
Bleeding
Hearts

Sara Sutton

authorHOUSE®

AuthorHouse™
1663 Liberty Drive
Bloomington, IN 47403
www.authorhouse.com
Phone: 833-262-8899

Published by AuthorHouse 03/17/2022

ISBN: 978-1-6655-4217-3 (sc)
ISBN: 978-1-6655-4219-7 (e)

This book is dedicated to my Mother Janet Lee Sutton.

Contents

Introduction

"Epiphany"

The Sun's heat is relentless, like the insatiable thirst of mosquitoes and my mind's unwillingness to rest. I am here, after years of torture. After years of brittle ice breaking me down to shreds, sharp as glass - my hands grasping at edges. My hands are now bloody but they still wrap their fingers around the fruit of life, and squeeze. I was dragged through the thorns because this time, my spirit wanted to be strong. I needed to be kneaded like bread; shaped, bent, coalesced. This breaking, bending, merging - somehow landed me here.

It happened at Summerlake Hotsprings, in Central Oregon. Just as the fire line of the sun burned its way along the horizon. The blind red rays shot my retinas like lightning and hit the thin flesh of my lids with more force than any morning before. My pupils retreated, shocked at how violent the sun raided my cabin, devouring every inch of space. Too much for my eyes to take in all at once, I had to slowly usher the light in, little by little so my iris' didn't explode. I had never been to the desert before that.

I had not realized how much the hills and mountains and trees block the sun from showing its full face. I, of course, had my own love affair with the sun, but never like what happened that sunrise. Looking around I immediately felt I had been lied to, forsaken, withheld from the only light that mattered, the only light that lasted. I had been bitterly betrayed.

The perfect sand colored curtains allowed the yellow mixed with red genesis like glow to flow in the stucco house and over its accents of weathered wood. My feet were on the cold stone floor before I even completely woke, unbalanced as I rose. I've never had a romance with the sun so crimson red. I've been captivated by it but never this fully, not nearly this entirely; it drawing my body out of the house, begging to kiss every inch of me and I too wanted to drink every inch of it. Drawn, not by something made of now but by something cosmic, eternal. Something cyclical.

And I felt something, as I opened the door to the vast and empty field, as the heat hit my skin - almost sizzling. Happiness on the needle point. Happiness concentrated. Connection, unfettered as I stood on the porch of the cabin watching the sun rise at 4:30 a.m. like an invasion; heavy troops marching steadily towards me as I stood and helplessly stared. The sun had never in my life woke me that early - that desperate for me to see its brightness, but that day it woke me and chose me because it knew how I like to be blinded, to be split open, burnt down to ashes.

I noticed a bite on my flesh- I looked down at the mosquito drawing my blood up its flute before I raised my hand to kill it and after I noticed the remnants of blood it left. And it hit me. Like the tiny and insignificant mosquito, I too must lunge towards any salty body of life and suck the blood until dry. Before something comes along to squish me out. Lately I have had words on the tip of my tongue, my thoughts perched on the edge of a cliff, ready to dive. My body gets older and my mind slowly unravels these questions I've sat on for years, returning to each night just for a quick check in - any progress yet? The unseen releasing to me only mere morsels of an answer, and mostly the answer is not articulated in any language, it's more of an understanding setting in, like how I finally understand what my mother meant when she said - cherish being young. Because now I understand that out here in this heat, not much can survive. The hour glass is stacking with sand, filling up by the second. Nothing in this world waits, and our flesh too falls from our grips like minutes, far before we are ready.

I brought my attention back and it occurred to me, I was the only one there awake. I wondered if the Sun made some terrible mistake, could it have arrived early - off schedule from a night of wild partying in the East? Quickly, I grabbed my towel, slipped on my sandals to step back outside towards the hot springs waiting for me, waiting for maybe a thousand years by now for that one moment in an entire planet's history. The silence was shocking, frightening, as if nowhere on earth was this quiet. As if any sound was wrong, other than the birds. Even in the fullness of day it felt disrespectful to talk, only wanting to usher a hushed whisper, scared to offend the grand cathedral of silence. I had no desire to take the attention away even for an instant, from what cannot be heard. All you could hear was the heat of the ground baking around you. And there was a comfort in the silence that is the exact opposite of loneliness. Like that silence was all you ever needed because in its presence every last mask fell away and shattered on the sharp rocks.

The sun was so aggressive in its approach but I was the only one on that savage yellow morning who could not sleep through it. It seemed more important than my tired mind cared to fathom - but waking alone and making my way to the hot waters was imperative. Vital. First. Something in me ached for healing. Ached for relief. Begged for answers or a glimpse of understanding - what is this life - what is this fire I am chasing? Can someone explain why I want to be fried by the electrical currents running through me; why I want more meaning than my mind can hold?

I arrived at the edge of the stone pool surrounded by the tall green grass. Allowing the moment to sink into me like I had always imagined. My skin predicted this. I took in the dampness of the rocks before the sun had the chance to warm them and I drank the sage sifting through the wind, viciously potent. I was naked, alone, about to dip into the hot spring and a bird fluttered and landed on the wooden post. Affirming that the answers will come if I give myself moments of diligent silence like this. If I travel for miles to places where the words are easier to find, where God is more present, where nature screams loudly. The heat of the sun laid an understanding in me like bricks - which said: the questions may never be answered, but the sensation of being alive is no less infinite, raging and wild. At night - in a place between sleep and dreaming - something tells you that someday you will die. And that you must use this time to drink up as much of the sweetness of life as your body can carry. Raise your hand and ask the questions. Ask the questions to yourself, to the desert, to the mountain, the ocean, the book, the friend. Ask anything and anyone who will listen. Suck down the marrow, soak in the dark earth's hot springs, and eat the sweet fruit that offers itself up to you so incessantly at your feet. If we are constantly lunging like the mosquito to lift the blood of life up our flute to our dry mouths, flying through the scorching heat of the earth - what more can we demand? What higher beauty can we imagine? There are millions of stars but we are *here* and the sun chose us regardless of the lack of chance. And the whole earth would freeze and die without this heat. This heat that melts away the pain in my ankles, the sadness in my ribs. The sacred water, emerging from the volcanic earth so the minerals can let my limbs float for a moment, for a moment not condensed with the weight of the death, the addiction. Not condensed with the weight - I become Re, Lugh, Liza, Apollo, feeling very much God-like in this life that is just one second. Pointing myself up or down to a single vision, verse or melody that lingers longer than all else. Asking - if I am to remember only one thing to bring with me at the end of my life - what is it going to be?

I am now content in my aloneness, in my unanswerable forebodings, feeling solitarily enough. Not harboring some great sorrow or languishing over lost love. If my bones want to come unhinged, if my veins want to close up and dry - I'm ready. I've been taught to drink the richness of each second, to proceed in the direction of the earth's magnetic pull, letting it lead me like a donkey to all the valleys and plateaus where my answers sit idly, forever evading me. Despite the evasion I can say this life is enough; my spirit flies - as a bird does through the smoldering heat - beating its wings fiercely up and down, up and down soaring towards the blazing light of the horizon. And what happens when the bird merges with the horizon of a wild fire like that? Do they survive - do they come out the other side? Or are they incinerated in the outburst of galactic heat? Are they as willing as me, to be burned in the wide open eye of the universe?

There are an infinite number of ways the light can fall on something beautiful. And we all see it differently. And that is life: the infinite ways in which light can fall and the infinite ways we chase it. Every one of us runs head first into a different flame, insatiably lost in blind passion - each fire burns at the same melting temperature. We all are burned up by what we love. Life was not designed to play out any other way. The flame is what we came for in the first place, it is what we want to be turned into. When they look at me I want them only to see my fire; what I came here to do. *My life* is about finding the brightest point on earth and staying there as long as I can. I go from one hot spring to the next, soaking my too young to be this sore bones, extinguishing my souls' sins from the last life, submerging my entire being in the scorched waters, knowing something inside me will rise up like the steam, and fly.

I let the silky water pour over my hair, face, neck, and breasts. I cannot convey the importance of this place in my story. The dire necessity for me to walk alone to the hot springs and soak for hours while all the others sleep so I can resurrect a part of myself that too, was sleeping. That night when the bat flew above the spring I was soaking in, another flew into my chest. All the commotion woke something. Something that told me to come down to the hot waters alone in my blossoming, to submerge my heart deep enough to wash away the ash from the fires I've ran through panting. From the panting came the smiling. Smiling, radiant, alone and my expanded mind enlightened in this bliss that is dancing. Maybe in an entire life, some only feel this for a few seconds. But I want it to be present in every breath. I hunt out these hot springs because I want to be scorched, burned, brought to smolder. I want to take what was never meant for me, what was always too good for me, I want to live so thoroughly that they have to scrape my happiness off the blacktop after its dried in the heat because it spilled over and out of me. I want to leave a scent, a mile marker, a chart of how to get where I am, a map to this happiness so others may find this place unscathed.

And the sun rose like lava; like there was nothing but light left in the entire universe.

Unboxing

I was a box
I had not unpacked
for years.
I was solely focused
on surviving;
no opportunity presented itself
in which to unload the trauma.
No space opened
to organize the drowning memories,
neither a scheduled hour to
catalogue the broken pieces
that collected at the bottom
of the box that is myself.
It was a luxury I could not afford.
And I know
there is no healing place,
no sanctuary
to unload the pain and *leave* it
by some rambling river.
There is this box
that is myself
that I use to carry the pain
and in the heat of my body
it slowly evaporates.

The Dark Bird

The dark bird of sunrise
attempts an approach,
perched on the shoulder of my life.
I've escaped her each time so far.
She risks everything
to try and ruin me.
But I know too much already
and she knows I would never
stop long enough
for her
to catch me.

Some Days

Some days I'm entirely depleted.
I don't want to give.
I don't want to take.
I just want to be.
A perfect night,
to me,
is a stunning sunset
and sitting silently
with a pen and paper.
How else can you see
what will come?
It's true -
you seek what seeks you.
You must take the step
to find
what's behind the breath,
what was always there,
careening ever so
slightly towards you
all this time.
That is how
love works
and poems
are written
and art
is made.

Talking

I was talking with him in the evening heat,
years ago
about past lives.
And what he read was that
our souls live forever and cannot die,
that our souls just keep being reborn,
until they reach unity with God.
And that we have something called a soul family
who we continually choose to be reborn with,
each life.

I said to him,
it makes sense now
why I wrote these lines:

I went through
so many lives
looking for you,
endlessly until now.

I have been walking
and searching
the eyes of lovers -
is it you?

It was a thousand years and more-
lives lived short and long.
I passed through towns, created families,
but my soul always waited up at night
for you to come for me.

I searched and found love
but it wasn't yours.
I died and searched again,
endlessly,
til the end.

Head of Household

I'm in the lands of Merl, Leonard, Cotton.
I fear a part of the world is dying,
wrinkling into nothing.
I fear memory is forgetting,
time, diminishing.
Every hundred years
we lose
and gain some;
creating our own fragile traditions.
But part of what survives should be left for dead
old hates, decayed beliefs,
outdated policies.
I've watched all the years of the world,
waiting for time
to open up to me,
to us.
Preparing for the evolving
that is now here,
coursing
through me,
through us.
We have taken our place
at the head of the table
and we did not ask permission.

Existing

Poetry is spilling out of me
landing everywhere.
Like a hoarder,
a pack rat,
I'm stacking words up in my closet.
There is now poetry on the ceiling,
the floorboards
the windows,
the door.
Some say you create the world
you want to exist in.
Well I want to live inside poetry.
I want my days and nights
to revolve
around the stringing together of words.
I want to exist in a room full of books,
I want to exist in a nook curled up
with the nostalgic glow of an evening lamp
and a record player softly singing out
the chords of a slow guitar.
I want to spend my life
in the far corner of all libraries,
digging
for another passage
that awakens a new territory of my soul;
uncharted and old.
I want to live inside poetry
and all conversations

I want centered around poems.
I want to live inside poetry
and every breath to be
spinning out poems.
I want to live inside poetry
as poets do.
Painting a world inside this one,
a universe of words to exist in;
my field of wildflowers in heaven.

Blue Hour

It is the blue hour again.
The blue blur.
Twice a day
the world turns
a deep blue.
In one quiet moment,
my hands on the counter,
breath out the window,
the earth fades to nothing
but a cold blue fog.
The fluorescent fog sinks
deep into the field,
until it is swallowed and resting.
I find the hour at both its openings.
I enter the delicate hour and linger,
as long as it will let me.
I will paint it,
(though I wish it could paint me).
I will paint the feeling so you can know
the vast everything and small nothing
the blue hour represents.
The vast nothing
and small everything.

Always

For My Love

I think this will always be us,
out into the cold air,
dogs in tow,
on a tree lined road.
It will always be us,
early morning cooing love songs to each other
across the feather pillows.
It will always be us,
and us alone
at the end of each night,
rubbing the soreness from each other's bones.
And us in the afternoon boredom, making the
mundane just a bit more bearable.
The house, though beautiful, can't hold us.
We are always off first thing in the morning,
out to find something
we can hold for only a moment,
then must release.

Creaking

My bones creak
like the tree.
I think happiness
may have left forever,
replaced by crippling anxiety
and the feeling
of always being lost in this world.
Nowhere feels like home
or is comforting.
Nothing offers the warmth
that my skin used to carry.
Now my entire body
has become a winter
that lasts forever,
a sun that just won't rise.
My mind,
a brittle smile
refusing to crack.
I am now taking on age
faster than I can bale
it out of me,
harboring hate,
mistaking judgement
and eating my own apologies.
I turn up the heat
and shiver
under the chatter
of my teeth.

The Preserving

When I'm asked
if I want children
I choke.
I feel like someone
is trying to trap me.
I've just escaped,
became free
yet again
you're trying
to cage me –
….so soon?
Instinctively I get up and run.
This feels like a set up -
my mind - a panicked flux.
Right now I do not
have it in me
to give.
I only have what it takes
to first fill myself up -
after a lifetime of
emptying.

Father

I swallow my thoughts
like a thick liquid
and
refuse
to
write
about
him.

The Releasing

I always stretch out
my legs
before I sleep,
to release
and set free
the negative energy
left over from the day
that became trapped
in the cell
of my body.

Head Trauma

I was not hit by him,
she was.
But
I
still
feel
the
impact.

Contemplating

If I lay a certain way,
I can
hear my heart beating.
So I quickly switch positions
to avoid the sound
that I,
in turn
become terrified of.
My mind toying around
with the fact that
someday
against my raging will -
the beat will
slow and
stop.

Waterfall

This process
is one of opening books
I closed years ago.
I can't say I'm ready
but I won't keep
holding on
to the talon
of this dark crow.

You brought us trinkets
you thought we'd like
during visiting time.
And we did.
Other kids
might consider it junk
but it came from you
with a smile
and your voice -
your voice
that said you loved me.
It was all I needed.

You were dirty those days,
after they took us away,
always smelling like cigarettes,
a lost puppy dog
look on your face.
And your eyes

that were crying
then laughing all at once.
And I
was always trying
to figure out
what secret hid
at the base of your heart.
What made you so empty
to want to fill your body
with such dark liquid
endlessly.
Why you were always looking
elsewhere
and never back,
at us.
Why you have always been
so impossible to find.
So out of reach.
So lost in love
with the prolonged
sense of numbness.

But there has been
no return call,
no retort,
not even an echo
in the empty woods.
And now

I exist
in a space that is
close to your
numbness;
a cold,
thick waterfall
of unanswerable questions
and in my palm -
a compass.

Opening

Some days it feels like I am not alive at all,
but set on sleep mode,
hibernating under the hum of a machine,
acknowledging but not interfacing.
Some days it feels like there is an hourglass in my chest
and all the sand is caught at the narrowest point
and sometimes the hour glass breaks
inside my chest.
Some days
it feels like maybe I do not know
what it feels like to really live.
As if there is a maple syrup of happiness
I have not tapped into yet
as in - others have found it but I haven't,
I see it on them.
Some days hunger could eat me alive
and end my life
all in one bite.
Some days I am the fog rolling in steadily,
making it impossible to see
others I am
the blue light just before dawn,
the fragrance that drifts on the pond.
Most of us know little, if anything
about how to live our lives.
About when to grasp at a celestial catalyst,
when to run and when to stay.
I look up to the sky

and hope it might open for me.
So that this feeling
of choking will leave.
Some days I wake up contaminated with sadness,
a grey light that says everything is meaningless
that life has no true purpose
but then comes a louder thought:
that I am all wrong,
and that surely it does.

The Dividing

I want to divide myself in two
and give you half,
I want to create half a being,
half a skin.
I want you in.
I want you always.
I want to meet for coffee
and say everything with a smile
and silently undress you with my eyes
in a crowded cafe.
I want to ask
if I can stay
with you
tonight
and I want you
to say yes.
Yes into this life
and the next.
My entire existence
while in their arms
I wished
they were yours
around me.

The Grand Cathedral of the Woods

My church
is the forest,
the river bank,
the ocean's shore,
forever
and
ever
and
more.

The Knowing

I found the words
I wrote -
years and years ago -
the lines that say -
I have always known.

The Reincarnating

There is so much I want to do.
Study the stars,
create art,
teach poetry,
build the house.
I want to drink more life
than this short clock
allows me time for.
Maybe that is why
we are given so many lives,
given try after try.
For finding what makes
our heart beat the fastest
so we can swim
the endless universe
towards
the center of that.

The Numbing

It's terrifying
not to feel.
To selectively
sever your emotions
from your perception
in an instant,
for as long as necessary.
A trained mind
can be scary;
after a while
of such dedication
to detachment,
you lose the ability
to feel at all.
You experience a numbness
that you can't find your way out of,
you are the cat with the paper bag over its head.
And there is only one reason for this:
it is easier this way - to forget.

Rumi

When the panic threatens
like glass crashing
on stone
I remember
that I am at home in myself.
I took his words very seriously:
all true wealth sits balled up
at the base of my spine.
He taught me better
than to submit to anxiety;
when the screaming finally stopped
I hid in my room and read his words,
threading them from ear to ear.
How am I in love with someone
who died 800 years ago?
A part of God died with him,
I am aching for the resurrection.

The Show of Strength

These days
us women
aren't replacing our last name
with our men's.
We keep ourselves
and add them to us
with a hyphen.
So we can
throw the identity
off like a purse
as we need
if they start the cycle
of mistreatment.
So we can pick them
from us
like a scab.
We are a new breed
of women:
enough within.
We are the bud, root and the stem.
We know
we don't
need
them.

Pulsating Murmurations

The drawstring of my mouth opens
and I speak of Starlings.
How they swarm in synchronized air shows;
pulsating murmurations.
How earnestly planes have tried to replicate them.
They remind me of mid-day laughter in the library,
stifled at first then expanding.
Whimsical, innocent notions nose diving from the
power lines downward until,
inches from the ground -
they twist up,
up with the fast wind that is soft
(only sometimes)
soft (this time)
as the freshly ploughed earth they land on.
Their chatter disturbs the silence of non living things,
the birds parading their beating wings -
a thousand pumping hearts floating through the air,
encased in black feathers.
The Starlings, so absorbed in their dance,
see themselves only in relation to each other;
acting as one connected body of water,
a flowing river in flight.

Ugly war

My bones are a chalky white consistency-
a smashed slab of marble,
brittle as glass between teeth.
Shrapnel got caught in my neck, it felt like
while trying to shed a skin that cracks
then crumbles.
Life is a dried leaf in my palm as
unforgiving fingers close around it.
The broken pieces float
with the rubble from the bombs
that crashed heavily
into the innocent heart of
citizens and their villages.
We wanted to believe it was for democracy
as the blood dripped thickly,
and the oil flowed steadily.
A good cause,
an eagle calls -
my thoughts
and the earth
fall back together
at the edge of the pond.

The Greatest Honor of My Life

At a restaurant tonight
to the right of me,
sat a woman
who reminded me of you.
I shifted uncomfortably in my seat,
unnerved at the slightest etch of you.
Only because the thought that you're gone
still blocks the light
like a full eclipse of the sun
and the great wide universe turns dark
when I remember
your voice has left the Earth forever,
your tired eyes
are no longer here to search.
In them: a light I had hoped to capture
before it was gone.
I would trace your bulging veins,
like a river on a map,
wondering if the bruises hurt.
I asked if I could brush your hair,
you smiled with your eyes closed and said yes.
Just to brush your hair,
was the greatest honor of my life.

Chasm That Pulses

It is programmed in our coding
to love.
To be a chasm that pulses,
a mouth dripping with pleasure
sucking in air.
We are the eye that opens,
the iris that holds its point.
Centered, like all the planet's -
impossibly perfect.
But it's all an accident, some say.
What are the chances?
That we are all,
every one of us,
some impossible,
miraculous mistake?

Late May, Early June

The ferns speak
their own peculiar language
this time of year.
The sun casts a more golden hue on them,
as if all sadness took a vacation,
as if only life existed
and no death.
As if the sky favored them somehow;
their spiraled fiddleheads reaching.
The sun leaves its red mark,
the rock face drenched, hot as fire.
The light leaves an orange haze around you,
and your whole world, for a flash of an instant.
The Dogwoods and Scotch Broom
tell me what time of year it is:
late May, early June.
And the clouds, sinking down
tell the secrets
God told them
not to.

Silent and Wild

Abstract poetry,
abstract mind,
my abstract world
unsatisfied.
I ask myself
what are you seeking?
Myself replies:
mostly places,
silent
and
wild.

A message to Society

I don't care
how hard you try
to make me believe
my lips are too thin,
my butt and boobs are too small,
or that I'm not quite tall enough.
You can try to convince me
I'd look so much better with my hair
a different color
but I just won't listen.
Because my guard is already up,
I've been watching you,
how you try to change people
and I'm playing defense, looking ahead,
looking deep.
Making sure I keep her, truly her.
I won't let any knives get close
to cut me up to their standardized bra size
or try to change my personality to fit their mold:
soft spoken, polite.
The trouble is –
I'm a bit loud,
my laugh reaches heights.
My feelings write themselves on my face
and that won't change.
I don't know how to be anything
but me
and at no time in my quick existence

do I plan to be.
Yet modern-day beauty standards are trying to
rape me of who I am
and make me
hate me because I'm not pretty - enough.
But
that tactic won't work on me.
I learned a long time ago
that the desire to change yourself
cannot arise from self-hate,
it must arise from *self-love*.

Expecting

This world isn't what I expected.
I see the point of being positive
but
it is a lie sometimes.
We are so hungry for
what we never had;
a life of ease and grace.
I expected good things,
but she had a different plan for me.
Or maybe fate is a he,
because a she couldn't be that cruel.
I was born into a world where
the entire earth is a mystery,
impossible to solve.
I'm not used to that part,
I require logical explanations.
Our hearts are flexible, yes,
like rubber under pressure
but sometimes,
the rubber band snaps;
a heart collapse, an avalanche.
To trust anyone is very kind.
Naive, beautiful and kind.

The Falling into Nothing

I.
The days pass by so quickly
without distinction.
It feels wrong to not
have achieved some goal.
It feels wrong to not
put my whole soul
into everything I touch.

II.
The day passed by so quickly.
Did it even happen?
It was one blink.
And it's all gone.
Everything that ever came before
now, now, now
is gone.
And we work, work, work
so hard, for so long
for one day to fall back
into nothing again.

Surviving

I beg myself to forget
about your absence for a little while
purely for my own survival.
I push down the thick
chalk of sorrow
like a heaping garbage pile.
Placing it far enough
away
that I cannot smell
the rot.
You can call it avoidance
but I swear
its' not
it's my way
of staying alive.

Outside of My Body

My bones don't sit the same today.
I'm outside of my body
looking in -
monotone, emotionless.
It all happens,
the song goes on
but I'm not there,
not here,
not anywhere.
I'm absent, tardy,
hardly conscious.
I am suspended in the space
between me and my dreams,
reaching -
fingers stretched out desperately.

Dusting

I'm surprised
how much dust
has covered you
in such a short
amount of time.
I wish I could
make you new,
erase the past,
wipe you off.
But you lie dormant
surrendered to
this life's failures.
The dust settles
faster than I can clear it.

Snapping

I could turn cleaning up for you
into a full time job,
if I were thorough.
I could make
a pretty little housewife for you;
swollen, hollow.
But how utterly miserable
I would be.
A caged bear,
a silent scream.
Death approaching on the inside
but outside I'm alive.
I snap to attention,
obedient, polite.
No, no –
I couldn't be
your miserable little housewife;
I bare my 4-inch claws
and tear this whole place
to shreds
instead.

Doing Circles

I wanted to write
a letter to you
but where
would I send it to?
Your death
won't make the news.
How do I know
if you're
even alive?
I'm trying to see
but I'm blind.
My hope no longer
has wings
and my sight
remains in stark blackness;
no light.

The Solitude

My work is of a very solitary nature.
I find myself apologizing
because I need to be alone,
need to cut out, head home.
Even food becomes an annoyance
when I'm in the thick of it,
creating.
Debating how I can become
even more
reclusive,
elusive.
My single pointed focus:
express the center.

The Fasting

The adoration –
a forbidden flirtation.
The sudden exploration of an
unexpected awakening.
The sensation –
is a variation of curiosity
and hunger
for a challenge,
a match,
a balance.
Starved for
this connection
never felt with anyone else
a silent instant recognition,
a certainty higher than self.

This is the one
I went through
all of my lives looking for,
without you
I will die only
to search more.

The Doubting

Coldness builds itself in you.
And there are leaves
that tremble
quite like you.
What happens
when you keep
piling the broken pieces
on top of each other?
(I'm telling you)
they cannot
hold out much longer.
I feel the weight
and it's crushing my bones.
Even my teeth, I feel them cascading
out of my mouth when I dream.
Falling away like the rest of me.

Am I not strong enough?

Finding an Exit

I dreamt a few times
that I stood on my tip toes,
body lifting off the ground
a few inches -
floating,
suspended
in air
just barely.
The
weightlessness
was
as real
as being awake.
I wished that
I could exist in
that world instead,
in a place *where
the heaviness
finds an exit.*

The Teachings

We have breath so we can speak.
Your silence is close to death.
Well, it's pouring rain,
we're driving,
and I see Mr. Z.
Long yellow trench coat
thought he'd go for a walk
in the rain.
His wife
all kind
would teach me of Christ.
On her wall,
a painting of a lighthouse,
cold grey sky, the beach.
Outside the house
across the street
lay the sea.

The Pleading

You resemble the black holes
in space:
raging, devouring, annihilating.
Filled with dense darkness,
no day seeks you.
Never would a single sun ray
want to reach you.
So many people
warned you,
begged you,
tried to save you.
But how can
someone so lost in love
with numbness
feel anything
or hear the whisper
of a child
who only knows how
to see
the light.

The Pulsing

Never forget
the heart is the first
organ of the body
that develops in the womb.
It's as if God were a poet too.

Belonging

The wooden flute begins
and I am taken back
again
to the forest
in my mind.
Wet earth, hot earth,
bare footsteps
in the dirt.
Slow movements
through the trees,
observing the way
stillness roams through the wild.
Something in us feels
an urgent intimacy
to the silence at the center of trees.
As if we once dwelled here,
existed as the bear, fox, deer.
The nearness is vital,
primal.
Our need for the wild
is undeniable now.
Even science tells us
the green colors of nature are calming,
the terpenes in the pine trees
benefit immune function.
And I am sure now,
my snout bent
to ground
of the Wolf I once was.

The Hoping

If I could
I would
scream all the voice
straight from my chest.
I would scream to you
on bloody knees
until my hoarse and broken voice
spread your name across the seas.
Scream until I'm split in two
broken and left with nothing
but wounds.
Short of breath and rivers of tears
from eyes of green.
My heart on the concrete is all you see,
faintly beating and slowing at increased speed.
And just before God reaches down
to extinguish the candle barely lit –
I whisper my love to you
and hope you hear it.

The Conversations

Each night I sit down
with my God.
We talk of current events.
We talk of the death,
the prescription,
the addiction.
We talk of how things
could have went
if the cards had been dealt out
different.

The Fear

I want to suck
the marrow
from the bone of life,
to leave no stone unturned.
I want my spirit to burn,
my blood to pump.
I want my mind to run.
I never want to stop
I never want to slow.
And if only
for a second -
I want to know
how it feels
to be
unafraid
to die.

Treading Water

I owe everything
to the sound of the rain;
I am sure
I could not have
survived this life
without it.
On all the nights
I told my thoughts
to eat themselves,
to drown -
the water ran beside me,
drank me up,
poured me out.
As long as there was breath in me,
I could swim.

The Sinking

My heart lives in a salt flat,
slowly sinking always.
My heart lives under a wave
quickly crashing always.
They think I'm Jesus,
That I can resurrect the dead.
That I can reverse the
damage done by a needle point.
I have pulled them by the hair
back up for breath
my fist full of coarse silk
that at one time was soft.
Unwashed, overgrown and stinking of tobacco.
Their hair reminds me of all the places
I don't like to be, the places they make me
come looking for them.
She said on Christmas
she walked the streets of Seattle,
with nowhere to go
and
even we told her no.
The pain doesn't settle, like dust.
It remains thick and poignant.
I'm just trying to learn how to swallow it
and keep it down.

The Wading

We waded waist deep through the creek
to fish for salmon.
I was trying
to pull something dying
out of the water
that was not my family for once.
I was trying to forget
how hard it has become to swallow.
So much is coming back up,
not wanting to be digested, processed.
My life regurgitates itself onto my lap.
I stare down at it,
disgusted at the smell,
like the catheters filled with urine
in the hospitals hopeless souls go to die.
We head for home
with the net full of salmon on my back.
It was a long walk in the sun,
I kept dipping them in the creek,
not wanting the meat to spoil.
Where I come from food is not wasted,
pennies are saved in the jar.
We were poor, born of parents who made
poor decisions,
parents who were not loved enough,
parents who wandered off
into the lonesome woods
and never came back for us.

The Lying Down

I looked out at the sun-drenched valley
scattered with trees and thought,
I want to lie down on that grass
and soak up whatever is there.
And suddenly I felt a thick liquid
being poured onto my chest
(I've always confused light for liquid)
as if someone were standing over me
pouring honey sweet nectar
onto the open wound of my heart.
My whole life I've been holding my breath
waiting for the release of pressure
and have yet to feel the weight lifting.
What I imagine is
a returning,
a bliss only nature can bring.
What I imagine is
the feeling I get
in dreams where I am flying.
What I imagine is
a sight so striking
it reopens the chasm of my sternum
with lightning,
lacing the pain with silver lining
to then stitch me back up again,
so be it if
the seam is jagged as a cliff.

The Dying

When we die
we do so without noticing.
But there is the sound of crickets,
the croak of frogs,
the smell of linen,
a window open.
On a night full of stars
we drift off
into the steady rhythm of frogs
like a drumming heart.
We feel comfort in their noise
knowing that we
are the only thing that ends
and our ending is really
not an end,
in this place
where there
are only beginnings.

The Work

After working 50 hours this week,
I come home,
cook dinner,
wash the dishes,
fold the laundry
and rub your feet.
Then I have
nothing
left
for
me.

The Watching

I've watched you die and come back to life
over 20 times combined.
You've got scabs on your face again,
dead giveaway.
This time, even on your back -
you've picked the scabs
and the blood leaks through your shirt.
You keep picking yourself open,
creating a more infected wound.
It's an itch you can't **not** scratch.

I live with the depression
as if we were room-mates
I don't try to sedate it
or run from it
(anymore).

Navigation

I point behind me and say "old home"
I point in front of me and say "new home"
I point to myself and say "forever home"

The Gentleness

I want to be as gentle with my body
as the dog is when licking its wound.
Caressing the dirty, jagged cut
with its soft wet tongue,
saying silently to it, *you'll be just fine*.
Speaking still with the tongue
but without words.
The tongue says: *you will heal
over time*.
Head bent obediently
down towards the wound,
submitting to it,
the dog lapping at the tear in the flesh,
comforting the weakness.
Mindlessly the dog heals itself,
having only
the instinctual urge to clean the wound
(not like us, who lather ourselves
in self loathing, unworthiness).
I tilt my tongue towards the gash
and know what I must do.

The Vengeance

I woke up spitting venom,
feeling more Medusa
than Mary
at the moment.
So what if I am
a wicked witch
a bitch,
too loud,
too blunt.
I know what you are thinking
the word is on
the tip of your tongue:
cunt.
That's what you want to call me
or any female that challenges
your authority.
Well you're lucky because today
I am feeling extra angry.
I could go over slowly
all the ways
in which
I've edited myself,
cookie cut myself out
to be what you want.
I could talk softly,
I know you don't like it
when we raise our voice to you,
or dare to argue.

I know it catches you off guard
to be told no, you're wrong -
but I've surpassed the last straw
breaking point -
holding my breath
and tongue for far too long.
Don't ever make the
the mistake again;
our purpose
was never to please you.
And we are not sorry.
We are strong.

The Collection

I've got poems collecting
under my nails
along with the
earth and blood.
The poems are oozing,
dripping
seeping
inking themselves out of me -
it's a bright thick liquid,
orange mixed to red.
I may not have birthed children
yet
but what does flow forward
was housed in the same cosmic fluid;
amniotic -
bringing with it
the same pride.

The Fragility

How fragile - skin,
like the intricate webbing and
composing of my thoughts -
materializing and deteriorating
in an instant.
Both will wash out to sea with the tide,
in time.
What is empty must be filled,
what's liquid must flow and soak
and what is open must
be closed.
Today or tomorrow -
the corner must be rounded,
the knife sharpened -
before the heart hardens
before God comes
and takes what is hers.

The Screaming

From thoughts
that scream louder
than asteroids
colliding in space.
To depths of quiet –
level upon level of silence.
Finding something false
with no escape
and no intended mending of hurts;
words empty.
I reach to touch you
and how could I not?
Like light on trees
why can't I just surrender to what is?
To a half love and a hole in my heart.
I want wind like the trace
of a hand on a face.
And shouldn't we try
for time to pass slowly -
without conversation?

Making Sense

I cannot make sense of so much.
I cannot make sense of emptiness
or wholeness. Of what is as real as thirst.
Or what's as deep as blood.
I'm trying to make sense of why
I am lying in bed on a summer day.
I'm trying to make sense
of everything that's falling,
all at once,
of what it means to hold someone.
I'm trying to make sense
of what everyone is not saying;
interpreting complete silence,
dissecting chaos.
I'm trying to make sense
of this feeling in the pit of my stomach.
Why I feel nervous, or anxious
or entirely unfulfilled.
What is this?
This inexplicable
feeling of loss.
A constant returning
of memories unsettled,
stirred up like leaves;
tracing my life
from open to closed.

The Building

Your hands
have known everything
closer than you.
Ask - what builds itself
upon your hands?
These are my hands.
And though they are not soft –
they are strong.
Even with dirt under my nails,
they are strong.
They gather what is needed,
heal what is wounded
and speak in a language
of no words.
They begin and they
end worlds.
These are my hands.
And even though they are
already wrinkled,
they hold the quiet river
that is my life, without
spilling a drop.

The Moving

Shouldn't we always
be moving towards
deeper levels of knowing?
But I don't know this part.
I don't know how
to see through your absence.
Your lost soul –
the mystery I was never
meant to unfold.
There won't be any
lightning strike of
the mind on this one.
Only the slow burn of
a candle down to wax,
an hourglass
almost out of sand.

The Fluidity

I stand facing
the first warm summer wind,
wondering where the light will fall
and strike the dark
on the thick way to the eyes.
We share a small room
with a small bed.
Our lives scattered,
bleeding into each other.
I try for a fluidity.
I sleep when you sleep
and wake when you wake.
And I wait.
This happens every summer
and I still
am lost
in this place.

The Women

We women,
we realize not the warrior within.
We are warriors just like men.
We have battled in wars of the heart
far heavier than any physical pain.
Our character is modest in its strength.
Gathering it slowly, silently, methodologically.
Building our spirit in subtle honor, becoming
and reclaiming the fierce
and potent urgency
of our sacredness.
Women, listen -
no longer
can we be denied
the truth
of our persistence.

The Piercing

There is a heaviness in my heart
that just won't quit.
A sadness deeper and wider
than any vocabulary can
articulate.
It is a punctuated pain,
piercing the most tender chasm
and never releasing.
Like a wounded animal,
I collect it then feed.
Believing
it will make my character
unfaltering,
deliberate,
consistent
and
never weak,
knowing only now
how to transform the pain
into strength.

The Found Language Poem

In Columbia 50 years ago
I was made with pearly whiteness.
Where strawberries are sold
by the yard.
They turned out early
with the 5 cents worth of tuna and edible tuber.
I met a wayside beggar
with some sample food stuffs
of the Northern Andes,
fetching the days' supply of water at the tavern.
I thought him a relic of colonial days.
Herds grazing along the edge
of the road
reminding me of men who go down
into the sea of pearls
only to find that the shark charmers
has lost his job.
Then homeward bound at sunset,
with the pearl oysters inside the bag
and the King's ransom in the palm of my hand,
soft parts covered by a skin.
We are the seekers
and the parting of ways,
on freight cars
and a camel train.

The Asking

I used to ask my mother,
how could I make her happy
as she lay bruised
and crying in my bed.
With the little strength
in her left
she turned to me
"you are my happiness"
she said.

The Bleeding

The body bleeds
the back aches
and the dog sleeps
with me
at the edge
of the fire.

The Dissolving

When I stretch out at night
I break down the anger
like sugar in water.
I let it dissolve.
Without any hesitation,
I obey my mind
because it protects me.
It matters not
how connected I am
to that anger,
or how badly I want
to hold onto it.
I have trained my mind
to soften the anger,
I have showed it
the sugar dissolving
in water and said,
"like this."

The Opening

In between the time
the sun rises
and sets
I will live like an animal;
my claws sinking into the
flesh of life,
ripping it
open
open
open.

The Inspiration

I'm in the woods again.
How do I
always
end up
here?
Inside us
are all the things
we never want
to escape us.
We want the deep green silence
to lie down in our soul
and stay forever.
We want to dwell
in so many moments
simultaneously;
how can I drink all of my sweetest memories
at once, elongating them,
preserving them like jam?
I have come to the woods again,
perhaps this time I will find
the crescendo
I have been pressing
ever forward,
searching for.

The Dancing

My spirit broke itself in two
and flew off
in yesterday's wind.
My heart is sitting at the bottom of a pond,
the earth beats a heavy pounding.
I want to be one
I want to be whole
I want to be full of iridescence
I want to have questions
even if they don't have answers
I want to wake up
from this
turbid nightmare
with the spirit of a dancer.

The Stealing

So we get in the car
and drive passed the hawks,
passed the alder,
passed the geese feeding in the field.
It's everything,
stealing away like this.
We should be working,
but we took to the afternoon instead.
To let the butterflies free for a while,
then back into the stomach
where they cocoon.
Work will be there when we return.
But you cannot say that for the
hawk,
the geese,
or this sweetness
in my mouth.

The Wondering

A song came on that reminded me
of you.
Death claimed your body at 17.
I can't imagine what it is like to die.
All I know is how to be alive.
How to be breathing, waking, living.
We used to sit in your car
and listen to this exact song,
dancing like idiots.
But now when the song ended
I wondered –
am I supposed to go on
breathing,
waking,
living
like I did
after they turned your flesh
to ash and put it back
to the ground?
Like I
woke,
lived
and breathed
after the overdose,
after Mom's funeral?
Now that it is done
do I go about my business
as usual?

The Blinking

I want to see what the raven sees,
as its wings swoop
through the half cloud
half mist
hanging low in the trees.
I want to feel the moisture
on my cheek.
I want to fly low,
I want to sit perched,
talons gripped to branch.
I want to know
that I was close
to the dampness of earth,
and the heat of the dirt.
My porcelain skin
absorbing the warmth,
letting it melt into me,
burning me to a smolder
so my bones can finally get
what they've always wanted,
to be turned back to the wild.
To be wide eyed
and slow blinking
like the doe.

The Emptying

I am emptied each night
and left each morning
with a desperate thirst for life.
Reset by default, my bliss is cyclical.
The sun burns every day at
the same scorching temperature
in the same way that I do,
without fail.
I can't help it, or what happened.
I still wake up thirsty for more
ready for life to dance with me,
happily releasing the grief.
Ready to narrow it down to a pointed answer,
the pinnacle, peak, climax.
I wake up parched each morning
knowing I want more
than I could ever possibly hold.
But isn't that what being human is -
desire growing from desire,
a spiral that never ends?

The Creating

Some of us birth children,
some of us birth
art,
music,
poetry,
structure,
recipes,
policies.
It's so very similar;
they are all screaming
on their way out
into the world.

The Obedience

I'm worn out
like the sole of an old shoe
offering myself up as a doormat,
so you can have something
to wipe the dirt onto.
How can I help
I ask,
what can I do?

The Ending

I exist alone
in the end,
I know that.
I think we all
quietly know that,
we just don't want
to think
it
too
loudly.

The Tracing

I trace the cracks in the wood
soft bark turned hard –
the knots are darker than the rest.
I wish I could be that still,
that quiet,
as patient as the knot.
Ancient Chinese teachings claim
there are humans with wood personalities.
Now I understand
why I want to be a tree
so badly.

The Understanding

I understand the world better through poetry.
It offers me an explanation,
an out breath - an exhalation.
I need it like bread.
I want it to wash over me like sleep
at bedtime.
I want it to drown me.
I want my nostrils to breathe poetry,
to feel it sliding down my throat
like a cold liquid.
I want to exist inside and outside of it.
I want to be surrounded.

I have found
the summit,
center and seed
of life
in poems.

Endlessly

Life has not
been gentle with me
but still somehow
my spirit wants to dance
endlessly.

The Shrinking

Society –
you tell me what to say
you tell me what to think
you tell me what to eat
until everything
about
me
shrinks.
And instead of myself
is the stench of conformity,
the act of absorbing
all the things
society thinks I should be
until I am a full sponge:
squeeze from me
who I am not.

Unspeakable

How do you return innocence to a child
after something like that?
He waited until the timing was right,
a young girl walks into the bathroom at a McDonald's,
proceeds to one of the stalls.
He walks in behind her, locking the door.
When she exits the stall
she is confused,
scared,
frantic,
....raped.
There is violent banging
on the outside of the door suddenly,
he opens it, saying:
"I was just washing my hands."

Bubbling

You call asking for money again,
you've lost it all,
how many times now?
Each time you fall from grace
the smack when you hit the ground
gets more deafening.
We all wring our hands on the sidelines,
anxiety bubbling in our stomachs like acid.
Watching you peel your mangled
musty flesh off the ground
we wonder
will he make it?

With our eyes open in the dark
it's the same as them being closed.

Rooting

My body has never known a more familiar smell.
Each time my reverence deepens,
my devotion
is dug further into the ground,
into the roots,
rotting pine needles
and rocks.
My body has never known
more comfort in a welcome.
My body and mind receives it well;
an alchemical reaction triggered by the sapp in the
bark,
crunchy snow and the neon moss.
I feel the footsteps walk over me
from a thousand winters and summers,
roaming the valleys and mountains
as though nothing else in the universe
could be more important.
As if each life I was supposed to go one way
but always veered towards the direction of the woods,
as if I had not had enough of a thing
that never really was the same or changed -
only familiar.

Landing

The snow spreads
and the world falls
to silence
to its knees
on its head
from the overwhelming
absence of sound.
We are on the search for deer sheds
when the white clouds descend.
The snow grows deeper,
the flakes, the size of silver dollars.
I imagine
what it might be like
left stranded like this.
There may not be
a more peaceful way
to die
than under the branches of evergreens,
under the thick and luscious flakes of sky.
It may not matter,
but perhaps it would make sense,
all of life
in the last quiet moments of breath.
All my life's meaning
could be found
in the light as feather
wings of a bird
and its tiny feet
landing on a branch.

Pretentious

My dad called
said he's down to 2 crack hits a week.
I am sick of people saying my weight
is too heavy for them
when they're not the one carrying it.
Unfortunately for me, Karen,
life hasn't been a juicy peach.
For me it's been an unripe pear, sour and hard.
I get it though,
the world is so sharp
some days I put on a barrier too
and hide from it all,
trying not to get cut and bleed.
But I am not going to apologize
for my life being messy
and my modes of expression not being
as sophisticated
as the gibberish ridden poems that win prizes for their
complexity. I say things simply. I want to be clear.
I want to be understood.
My mother said she didn't like poetry
because she didn't understand it.
The pretentiousness of intellectuals
have tried to keep a certain type of person
(poor people)

out of their community by exclusion.
I showed her simple poems, some Mary Oliver.
She smiled and said she liked those ones.
I nodded and replied,
I thought you might.

Substance Abuse

They've been drinking all day since noon.
That is the perfect recipe for a tsunami - a typhoon.
He starts the fight by not liking something she said.
"What did you say to me?"
She must have used the wrong tone.
Uh oh.
He stands up now, asking again,
WHAT did you just say to me?
An inch from her face
his teeth clenched
he calls her a bitch, a cunt.
Blood boils, I snap.
I know where this leads,
I'm up now
shoving my body in between.
Surprised, he says to me "you ain't shit."
My fists begin to grasp at any contact point I can hit.
My 14 year old knuckles smashing against drunk flesh
until my brother pulls me away while I scream
"you touch her and you're dead!"

Eternally

I'll be there
at the end of time
when all this is through -
standing, smiling
waiting for you.

Seducing your Pain

It's a chemical reaction,
like something that once tasted
bitter but now is sweet.
Somewhat like water
changing forms
in different environments.
Similarly you
feel the pain and transform the energy
using these sacred techniques.
Not everyone understands
what this means.
Thankfully, not everyone
has had to bare so much pain
that the only choice left
was to learn to love it
and defeat it.
It thought it would destroy me
but I came out laughing.
Because I so easily
seduced the pain
and reduced it *to nothing*.

The Transformation

One me died
as another was born.
And it wasn't sad or bitter
or cold,
it was strong,
glowing and warm.

Let Love Rise

We are a new kind of being.
We bend when we are
supposed to break,
we live when we are left to die.
There is no question,
no doubt
from my toes
to my eyes -
we were put here
to push through
and let love rise.

The Healing

Water has healed me.
Hot shower,
hot tub,
hot springs,
hot sauna,
escaping to the sea,
a lake
a river
to quickly think
to breath
when all of life feels like a suffocation.
The heat scalds what no longer belongs.
And it heals the body while repairing the mind -
a damaged thing.
Water and heat have been my tool.
Like the earth I let it mold me,
break me
and open me
back up again.
But the truth is,
it will take lifetimes to heal this.

The Spoiling

I've worked so much this week
the meat has gone rancid in the fridge.
I catch a glimpse in the mirror
and know my flesh will someday spoil too,
there is an expiration date on this
suit I wear.
But not on what lies within:
ether, energy, atoms, the soul
what cannot be held.
Hold.
I hold the guilt of leaving you on your deathbed,
because work was waiting.
I carry the guilt
I carry it like a dagger
that I use to pierce myself
when the self hate grows thick,
asking myself
how do you think she felt,
searching the room for my eyes in her last breaths
to not see me there - her mind drowning in fear.
The least we can do for the ones we love is to hold their
hand as they float off into the darkness,
and I couldn't even do that.
And when everyone leaves
I lay on the floor
and sob,
begging her for forgiveness.

The Budding

I am young
and what I mean by that
is
I have not budded yet
I have not flowered yet
my wave has not crested yet.
I am the sun suspended on the horizon
refusing to set.
I am a river that has not flooded,
I am potential energy,
unrealized;
(an avalanche
waiting to fall).

Rounding

The most powerful things
we know are round:
paws, breasts, sun,
the earth itself, a cell.
What is the circle saying to us?
Something so loud
none of us have ever
been able to clearly
make it out.

Gravitating

The thing is,
with you -
our love was born
before the stars.
Our two souls were the first thing
God wanted to see;
in the beginning
it was just us three.
We seem to find each other
in this great wide universe -
our wild
child like smiles
gravitating closer always.
God set magnets in us,
so we could find our way back to each other,
even drifting, my mind always missing a piece of itself
in your absence.
Until I reach my completion in you,
the end of a 1000 year cycle,
my soul transcending densities to locate you.
Relying on the metal in the magnet,
before my blood pumps all the way through.

Pushing on

The grass pushes upwards
despite the rocks,
rising is a force
heaviness cannot stop.
The pressure against us
only makes us
strong.

Not Wanting

I don't have dogs
I don't have cats
I don't have kids.
I have nothing that binds me,
like the feet of the women
in the Song Dynasty.
All I have is an egg
that bleeds out every month
because it knows
it can't
stay here.

The Passing

I woke this morning,
not expecting the golden orb of the moon to be waiting
outside my house, casting a shadow, wide over the
earth.
Last night a thought came to me.
And it is a recurring thought.
But it feels more like a visitation of some sort.
It's a feeling, a vision, a dream like state that comes and
tells me that someday I will die,
to not get so used to this life.
The realization sinks in only right before sleep,
in the space just before dreams.
All our lives we see it happening all around,
and never think it will happen to us.
Until it does, and accepting the dust you will be turned
back into, is a lot harder without trust.

Flowing

The flow of the river doesn't stop or slow,
the river's rim heaves and bows.
I have yet to arrive at the crescendo of my life,
I exist in the constant state of ripening.
Falling at exactly the right time
to be devoured by the earth.
Back to mud, roots, back to stone.

The Fear

I don't want to love someone
so much
and have the possibility of ever losing them.
I've known that loss
too much already,
I made a home
out of it.
I've lived in the cavern,
the canyon;
gaping,
wide,
deep,
empty.
I won't go back.

Telling Myself

And every night after work
I tell myself
that I will organize my closet,
that I will write,
I will do art.
But I never do -
I'm always too tired
and I just keep getting older
and I am beginning to get ugly;
the savagery of aging.
The hair darkens,
the lines - are defining,
stubble thickening,
my back pain more dense.
Youth abandons you. Pities you.
Leaves you, so you can know what it is
to love yourself completely naked (if you can)
depleted of gloss, foundation, fashion.
But you long for it. Ache for it.
We all watch our youth slip from us
like a shadow slinking shamefully away,
onto the next young beautiful thing.
Its job here is done
as we call frightfully after it
"where are you going..."
replacing itself
with these purple lines on my legs,
an enemy I feel has invaded my body.

I want them erased,
annihilated.
How dare they trace upon
my upper thigh, inner thigh, outer thigh.
How dare age touch me.

The Searching

I.
I carved out an image of you,
pressed paint to it
and stamped it across the continents.
I say out loud – I'm looking.
I brought a piece of your clothing for the hound;
I'm trying to sniff you out.
A disciplined progression –
forward at first light.
Forever following the trail
lined with ferns.
Sometimes I stop to smell the air
wondering if you're still here,
still confined to this earth,
or if your spirit moved on
even though your body still roams
empty as the forest.
I get the feeling,
you can't be found.
The source of that feeling
shifts and adjusts
the load on my back
and heads me for home.
II.
There is a me that exists,
a shadow self
dwelling in the
moist body of the earth.

Hunched down on my haunches
waiting for an answer,
a return call from the dark bird of sunrise
or a sudden spark
of lightning in my mind.
It is all making sense,
the yearning for dense flesh,
for a sudden expanse of air into a mouth,
a heavy breath out loud,
a settling of stillness.
The moment I finally sit back exhausted
and laugh.
It was all meant to
break me open
so this liquid could seep out.
I was meant to be tapped,
like the maple tree.
So that the nectar
could drip steadily.
This vibrancy, this fluidity of thoughts.
III.
My life was one that needed explaining,
dissecting,
asking.
What am I here to learn or unlearn?
To drink in or vomit away?
Why has sorrow
run through me
like a river that leads
out to sea?

Finally
a voice tells me
stop looking, let it die.

The question goes unanswered.
The door of life closes
as I stitch my thread
through the night.

Artemis

I made this crown myself.
With feathers and shells,
flowers and stones.

I place this pinnacle
of pride upon my head
and know exactly
who I am.
Artemis; the Huntress,
the Goddess of the forest.

My soul craves
the call of the magpie,
the sound of river
and rustling leaves.
It is always the first
and the last
imprint in my mind.

I would come back
to Earth
1000 times
if I could devote
each second to our Mother
and the thirst
she creates in me.

As one reaches the top
of the mountain
only to ask,
what is beyond
the next ridge?

The Car Accident

Just last night,
I thought of things untouched.
Looked out the window
and felt the weight
of the heavy rain
as if it were on my own chest.
And it hasn't stopped,
not for a second.

The Wolf of Death

In the pitch dark forest
I sleep,
with the wolf skin
wrapped around me.

The wolf lives
inside my chest.
Don't rest,
don't rest.

The wolf waits until I sleep
then pounces on me;
a sort of training -
making sure I am ready.

The wolf waits
for me to tell her:
it's time -
my hair is grey, bones heavy -
devour and release me.

The Invisible

Something pulls you from inside,
like how the sail boat is pulled by the tide.
Like how the birds
know where to migrate,
and the fish - where to spawn.
The cycle itself is what we are seeking.
Certain seeds of trees won't grow
until they have been burned.
That is how we are.
Begging for the fire
to bring us to ash
and back to life.

Butterflies

I opened
up a space
inside my body
for the light
to come in
and because of that -
the butterflies in my stomach
still live.

Naomi

Can I sit
and read you poetry
like I used to,
my souls friend?
My heart and yours
are one.
The remembrance
of lifetimes together
lingers like our
wild laughter.
We used to
run through the night
drunk with youth, dancing.
Now my heart
hungers for those
nights;
unapologetically
lost in savage
happiness.

God knew
exactly what I needed,
when she sent me you.

In the Beginning

My spirit is a dancer,
ecstatically twirling,
in the universe of stars
moved, beyond control
by a spark-
the
beginning of all days.

Ritual

Each night
I anoint myself
with
sweet orange oil,
lemongrass,
lavender.
A mixture of devotion-
to the great mystery,
to the racing wind.
I press my hands together
whispering
a few kind words
to my sunken heart.
I breath in
slow
and deep,
and release.

I am

I am a divine being
realizing my own divinity.
Each day a new petal
of the flower
unfolds.

American Horror Story

I've been trying to find
a way to say this:
(the thought is dangerous
and yet)
my mind won't let
the words
come out of my chest.
What if I keep climbing?
Letting earth and blood build
under my nails,
letting earth and blood build.
He raped your girlfriend
as he held a gun to your head,
you stuck a needle in your neck
all on the same bed.
I try to erase
your black
track marks.
I try to
wash you clean.
I will keep climbing,
letting earth and blood build
under my nails,
letting earth and blood build.

Depression Deepens

The dark bird of sunrise
is becoming harder to escape.
I wake up devastated.
I turn my head
and see the bird perched,
determined.
I jump up and run.
Faster than I ever have before.
She's gaining on me;
I've gotten slower,
or her, faster.
She wants to destroy me.
She chases
and I run -
clinging to the light in my mind.
Begging myself
to never stop
to never slow -
bare feet
and dripping wet
lungs dropping,
gasping for breath.

Renouncing

My life consists
of rivers and streams
honey and bee's,
a forest full of bleeding hearts,
wild flowers
and eagles.
We must renounce
all Gods but the Earth.

Transcendence

I am the goat farmer
in the misty hills of Sardinia,
aging cheese
and my soul's intent
in the fire smoke.
I am the gypsy in India
charming snakes,
dancing in the night
with skin hot to the touch
and dusty feet.
I am the soldier in battle.
Running to keep alive,
and leaving the dead behind.
I am the deck hand,
the captain,
the sea
and the ship.
I am the shepherd,
the pasture and the lamb
within it.

Surrendering

My entire life
I've wanted
to crawl into a ball of light.
I surrender, life won.
I feel the pain you carry
and I want it to quit.
I want to shed it like a skin -
and turn my attention
to something more comforting,
something more alive.
The pain has run its blade
so deep through my life -
I've become desperate
to escape it, to evade it.
At times I can outrun it,
but only for a moment.
Then quickly
she's on me
again:
the dark bird of sunrise.
It's said everything happens for a reason,
and I'm just dying to know
what all this means -
this life,
my praying hands,
their needles thin.

Dancing

It feels like
my body is filled
with toxic waste -
and then
the music plays.

I can dance
on top of every
horrible experience
I've ever had -
stomping them down
into the thirsty ground.

With every twist
of my hips,
each flick of my wrist,
I throw off
the heart ache.
And like magic
the pain is gone.

And I dance -
with the butterfly strength
of all the women
that have passed
through this earth.

Printed in the United States
by Baker & Taylor Publisher Services